D0613010

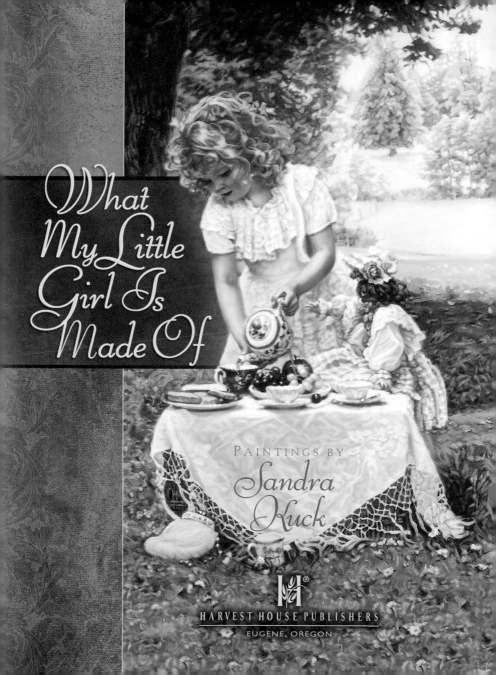

What My Little Girl Is Made Of

PAINTINGS BY

Sandra Kuck

HARVEST HOUSE PUBLISHERS

EUGENE, OREGON

What My Little Girl Is Made Of

Text copyright © 2005 by Harvest House Publishers
Eugene, Oregon 97402

ISBN-13: 978-0-7369-1447-5
ISBN-10: 0-7369-1447-1

All works of art reproduced in this book are copyrighted by Sandra Kuck and may not be reproduced without the artist's permission. For more information regarding art prints featured in this book, please contact:

> V.F. Fine Arts, Inc.
> 1737 Stibbens St. #240B
> Houston, TX 77043
> 1.800.648.0405

Design and production by Garborg Design Works, Minneapolis, Minnesota

All rights reserved. No part of this publication may be reproduced, stored in a retrieval system, or transmitted in any form or by any means—electronic, mechanical, digital, photocopy, recording, or any other—except for brief quotations in printed reviews, without the prior permission of the publisher.

Printed in Hong Kong

07 08 09 10 11 12 13 / NG / 10 9 8 7 6 5

What Is a Girl?

Little girls are the nicest things that can happen to people.

They are born with a bit of angelshine about them.

ALAN BECK

The Day We Met

*W*hen I saw your sweet face, I _____

_____

*E*veryone who met you would say _____

_____

*Y*our name was chosen just for you because _____

_____

*M*y hopes for my future daughter were _____

_____

*M*y first prayer for you was _____

_____

_____

Little girls are . . .

A sweet new blossom of humanity,

fresh fallen from God's own home,

to flower on earth.

WILLIAM MASSEY

The Gift of You

*Y*our presence in my life taught me to _____

_____

*H*aving a little girl changed my life because _____

_____

*E*very time I held you, my heart overflowed with thoughts of ___

_____

I thanked God for many things about you, but most of all for ___

_____

_____

_____

_____

_____

_____

_____

Often God's biggest gifts to us come
in the littlest of packages...our children.

ANONYMOUS

5

Beauty All Around

Your inner beauty was evident when _____

_____

_____

I was captivated by your beautiful _____

_____

_____

Colors, textures, and designs that attracted you include ____

_____

_____

Your room was decorated with _____

_____

_____

The outfit you loved to dress up in was _____

_____

_____

_____

There is a garden in every childhood,
an enchanted place where colors are
brighter, the air softer, and the morning more fragrant than ever again.

ELIZABETH LAWRENCE

A little girl likes new shoes, party dresses, small animals, first grade, noisemakers, the girl next door, dolls, make-believe, dancing lessons, ice cream, kitchens, coloring books, make-up, cans of water, going visiting, tea parties, and one boy....She is loudest when you are thinking, the prettiest when she has provoked you, the busiest at bedtime, the quietest when you want to show her off, and the most flirtatious when she absolutely must not get the best of you again.

ALAN BECK

A Day in the Life of You

Your morning ritual was _____

_____

_____

At mealtimes we used to _____

_____

_____

Almost daily you would talk me into _____

_____

_____

Bath time was always an adventure because _____

_____

_____

Our evening routine to lull you to sleep was _____

_____

_____

_____

Heart and Soul

You found comfort in _____

_____

_____

You said you wanted to someday marry ___

_____

_____

When you talked to God, you _____

_____

_____

The gifts of the heart you shared with others were ___

_____

_____

_____

Who would ever think that
so much can go on in the
soul of a young girl?

ANNE FRANK

Steps of the Journey

I always smile when I think of the time you _____

_____

_____

I cry when I remember _____

_____

_____

One of your biggest obstacles/trials as a child was _____

_____

_____

Pride filled my heart many times, especially when _____

_____

_____

A toddling little girl is a center of common feeling which
makes the most dissimilar people understand each other.
GEORGE ELIOT

You Say the Sweetest Things

Humorous, clever, or insightful things you have said.

Sandra Kuck ©2000

Scenes from Your Life

Tender moments through the ages.

When you were a newborn (cuddling, cooing, crying): _____

_____

_____

_____

_____

_____

When you were 1 to 3 (walking, talking, connecting with others):

_____

_____

_____

_____

_____

When you were 4 to 6 (making friends, going to school, playing):

_____

_____

Little girlie, kneeling there,

Lisping low your evening prayer,

Asking God above to bless me

At the closing of each day,

Oft the tears come to my eyes,

And I feel a big lump rise

In my throat, that I can't swallow,

And I sometimes turn away.

EDGAR GUEST

Legacy and Love of Family

The people who make your family include _____

_____

_____

_____

The family traditions you loved most were _____

_____

_____

_____

Our family pets were _____

_____

_____

You enjoyed family outings such as _____

_____

_____

_____

$\mathcal{I}$ can see the legacy of others in your face and personality.

$\mathcal{Y}$ou seem so much like _____

_____

_____

_____

_____

_____

_____

_____

A Few of Your Favorite Things

Favorite books/toys: _____

_____

Things that made you laugh: _____

_____

Favorite television shows or characters: _____

_____

Your ideal backyard would have _____

_____

Favorite animals: _____

_____

When I was in a hurry, your favorite stall tactic was _____

_____

Favorite music: _____

_____

A perfect day for you would include _____

_____

*F*avorite sports and games: _____

_____

*Y*our best friends over the years: _____

_____

*A*t one time you said you absolutely had to have a _____

_____

*F*avorite thing to do with your daddy: _____

_____

_____

_____

_____

_____

Pink bows and pretty things,
Fancy dresses and golden rings,
Little girl wishes and princess dreams,
She dances on stars and moonlight beams.

VERONICA CURTIS

I hear in the chamber above me

The patter of little feet

The sound of a door that is open,

And voices soft and sweet.

From my study I see in the lamplight

Descending the broad hall stair,

Grave Alice, and laughing Allegra,

And Edith with golden hair.

A whisper, and then a silence:

Yet I know by the merry eyes

They are plotting and planning together

To take me by surprise.

HENRY WADSWORTH LONGFELLOW

Laughter and Joy

Your favorite game of make-believe was ⎯⎯⎯⎯⎯⎯⎯⎯

⎯⎯⎯⎯⎯⎯⎯⎯⎯⎯⎯⎯⎯⎯⎯⎯⎯⎯⎯⎯⎯⎯⎯⎯⎯⎯⎯⎯⎯⎯

I could make you laugh by ⎯⎯⎯⎯⎯⎯⎯⎯⎯⎯⎯⎯⎯

⎯⎯⎯⎯⎯⎯⎯⎯⎯⎯⎯⎯⎯⎯⎯⎯⎯⎯⎯⎯⎯⎯⎯⎯⎯⎯⎯⎯⎯⎯

⎯⎯⎯⎯⎯⎯⎯⎯⎯⎯⎯⎯⎯⎯⎯⎯⎯⎯⎯⎯⎯⎯⎯⎯⎯⎯⎯⎯⎯⎯

You could entertain yourself for hours by ⎯⎯⎯⎯

⎯⎯⎯⎯⎯⎯⎯⎯⎯⎯⎯⎯⎯⎯⎯⎯⎯⎯⎯⎯⎯⎯⎯⎯⎯⎯⎯⎯⎯⎯

⎯⎯⎯⎯⎯⎯⎯⎯⎯⎯⎯⎯⎯⎯⎯⎯⎯⎯⎯⎯⎯⎯⎯⎯⎯⎯⎯⎯⎯⎯

Songs you liked to sing: ⎯⎯⎯⎯⎯⎯⎯⎯⎯⎯⎯⎯⎯⎯

⎯⎯⎯⎯⎯⎯⎯⎯⎯⎯⎯⎯⎯⎯⎯⎯⎯⎯⎯⎯⎯⎯⎯⎯⎯⎯⎯⎯⎯⎯

⎯⎯⎯⎯⎯⎯⎯⎯⎯⎯⎯⎯⎯⎯⎯⎯⎯⎯⎯⎯⎯⎯⎯⎯⎯⎯⎯⎯⎯⎯

The holiday you used to anticipate so early was ⎯⎯

⎯⎯⎯⎯⎯⎯⎯⎯⎯⎯⎯⎯⎯⎯⎯⎯⎯⎯⎯⎯⎯⎯⎯⎯⎯⎯⎯⎯⎯⎯

⎯⎯⎯⎯⎯⎯⎯⎯⎯⎯⎯⎯⎯⎯⎯⎯⎯⎯⎯⎯⎯⎯⎯⎯⎯⎯⎯⎯⎯⎯

⎯⎯⎯⎯⎯⎯⎯⎯⎯⎯⎯⎯⎯⎯⎯⎯⎯⎯⎯⎯⎯⎯⎯⎯⎯⎯⎯⎯⎯⎯

Sugar and Spice

I knew you were your mama's girl when _____

_____

_____

You loved to make-believe you were a _____

_____

_____

You could charm anyone when you _____

_____

_____

Your favorite girly things to do: _____

_____

_____

Your favorite tomboy things to do: _____

_____

_____

What are little girls made of?
Sugar and spice,
And everything nice,
That's what little girls are made of.

TRADITIONAL NURSERY RHYME

There was a little girl
Who had a little curl
Right in the middle of her forehead
When she was good
She was very, very good
But when she was bad she was horrid.

HENRY WADSWORTH LONGFELLOW

Only You

 $\mathcal{F}$ rom the beginning I could see that you were _____

_____

_____

_____

 $\mathcal{Y}$ our creativity was expressed in lots of ways, including _____

_____

_____

_____

 $\mathcal{Y}$ ou strived for your independence most by _____

_____

_____

_____

 $\mathcal{E}$ merging talents include _____

_____

_____

_____

Dreams of Becoming

$\mathcal{I}$ thought you might grow up to be a _____

because you always _____

_____

_____

_____

_____

$\mathcal{Y}$ou said you wanted to be a _____ some day.

$\mathcal{I}$ caught a glimpse of the woman you would become when _____

_____

_____

_____

$\mathcal{M}$y prayers for your future are _____

_____

_____

_____

_____

_____

The knowingness of little girls
Is hidden underneath their curls.

PHYLLIS McGINLEY

Growing Up so Fast

The day I realized you were no longer a baby but a little girl was

_____

_____

_____

To act older you _____

_____

_____

_____

I was proud of your courage when you tried to _____

_____

_____

_____

As you grow older, the most important thing to remember is _____

_____

_____

_____

_____

Don't let anyone think little of you because you are young. Be their ideal...be a pattern for them in your love, your faith, and your clean thoughts.

THE BOOK OF FIRST TIMOTHY

Sandra Kuck
© 2001

What Life Is Made Of

My Letter to You

_____

_____

_____

_____

_____

_____

_____

_____

_____

_____

_____

_____

_____

_____

_____

_____

_____

$\mathcal{D}$ear _____ ,

You are made of such goodness and gladness that my life overflows with wonder.

There are times I have given you my hand to offer support and comfort; I have given you my heart as a source of love and nurturing.

Now I give you my memories of your early years and offer glimpses of the little girl who reached for my hand, shaped my heart, and changed my life forever.

Love,